Table of Contents

The Starting Point Leader Notes are a critical component for leading a group through the Starting Point experience. These notes walk the group facilitator through special preparations for group meetings, provide a suggested flow for each session, and offer key questions to anticipate and address as the story unfolds.

For ordering information, please visit www.zondervan.com/startingpoint

The Starting Point Bible is a TNIV version of the Scripture text designed to complement the Starting Point materials. It contains special helps, including articles by Andy Stanley, book introductions geared to Starting Point participants, maps, and more.

For ordering information, please visit:
www.northpointresources.org/spbible

2

Design by INDUSTRY at www.designindustry.com.
Photographs used by permission from www.andrewmalec.com and www.istockphoto.com.
Copywriting by North Point Ministries and Kaleo Ranch at www.kaleoranch.com.
Line art Bible illustrations are from *The Dore Bible Illustrations* by Gustave Doré.
Cover Painting by Clayton Santiago; used by permission. www.renderedartists.com.

Soli Deo Gloria

Welcome to the Starting Point experience! Starting Point is a conversational environment where you can explore faith and experience community. In preparation for each group meeting, there will be a chapter to read and a few questions to answer in this Conversation Guide. Each chapter contains five components:

- **The Story Unfolds:** narrative introduction
- **The Story Behind the Story:** key Scripture text
- **Tensions in the Story:** thought-provoking question
- **Continuing the Story:** additional resources
- **Storyline:** the bottom line

There are also audio, video, or other experiential components to do each week. The group experience will be based on all of these elements. Therefore, it's important to complete them each week before your group meeting. In preparation for your first group meeting, please read and complete the questions for Chapter One.

When your group meets, discussion and dialogue will be a priority. Your leaders will not teach or lecture, but will facilitate conversation and seek input from all members. Plan to ask good questions and share what you are learning. Be respectful of others in the group. Listen when they speak and be affirming whenever you can. Above all, trust that God has led you here for a reason…

…to find your place in the story

The *Start* of Something NEW

I had always felt life first as a story: and if there is a story there is a story-teller.

~G. K. CHESTERTON

Our pursuit of God is successful
just because He is forever seeking to manifest Himself to us.

~A. W. TOZER

There is no greater agony than bearing an untold story inside of you.

~MAYA ANGELOU

CHAPTER ONE

STORY

The Start of Something New

We are lonesome animals. We spend all our life trying to be less lonesome.
One of our ancient methods is to tell a story begging the listener to say—and to feel—
Yes, that's the way it is, or at least that's the way I feel it.
You're not as alone as you thought.

~JOHN STEINBECK

All human beings have an innate desire
to hear and tell stories and to have a story to live by.

~HARVEY COX

THE STORY UNFOLDS

The Start of Something New

Your life is a story. It began the moment you drew your first breath. And the plot has been building ever since, adding new dimensions with each passing day. Your story is told through the pages and chapters of your life. As each scene unfolds, it reveals the meaning of the overall storyline.

Like any story, there are moments of clarity and moments of uncertainty. From time to time, you may find yourself struggling to remember where you were headed, and why. There are even occasions when you feel like you've lost your place in your own story. The pieces can seem fragmented. You know it's supposed to make sense somehow, but the chapters don't quite fit together. Something's missing.

And then one day, you discover the true context for your story… that your story is part of an even bigger story. Suddenly, the events of your life begin to fall into place. And with a new understanding of your past, you face the future as if starting all over again. *This is your starting point.*

Everybody has a starting point… the moment when you first sensed the presence of a grand story in your life and began to see the chapters of your life against the backdrop of time. Perhaps it was the birth of your first child, the death of a loved one, or a time of crisis when you called out for help from whomever was "out there." For others, it may have been the influence of someone else who was a little further down the road.

YOUR STORY IS PART OF AN *even bigger* STORY.

Where did it begin for you?

Were you raised with a belief in God and a sense of your own spiritual destiny? Or was God a vague concept that only came up on a few rare occasions? No doubt you know the experience of lying in bed at night and wondering what life is all about. But depending on your upbringing, God has either been a big or a small part of your worldview. In fact, if we're honest with ourselves, most of us got our primary image of God from whatever we were taught growing up. If you were raised in a religious environment, you probably tend to see God through the traditions and practices you experienced in your church or family. And if you weren't a "church" person, your picture of God has been shaped by your observations of the world, your education, your circumstances, and the influential people in your life.

Maybe you would describe this as more of a "turning point" than a starting point. As you connect with God, the course of your life seems to be moving in a new direction. Or, if you're getting back to the spiritual roots of your childhood, you might find the term "returning point" more accurate. By joining this group, you're hoping to connect with others and reconnect with your faith.

Or, perhaps you've been here before, and "restarting point" is the best description. After all, no one outgrows the need to explore life's journey from a new perspective. Wherever you are, you're in the right place. In a typical Starting Point group, you are likely to be surrounded by all of the above. Together, we will trace God's footsteps through the universe and examine his fingerprints on your life.

Whatever your situation, this is indeed a starting point. Whenever someone expresses a new level of interest in God, he considers it the start of something new. Perhaps you're here because you are drawn by something you can feel.

but can't quite describe. Or maybe you have a gnawing question about God you hope to get answered. Perhaps you just want to join others on the journey. Whatever the reason, this is an important milestone as you set out to explore your faith and find your place in the story.

QUESTIONS FOR REFLECTION:

■ Would you consider this a starting point, a turning point, a returning point, or a restarting point? Explain why.

■ What role has God played in your story up until now?

THE STORY BEHIND THE STORY ■ ⟶

Each week, we will examine the Bible, a source of spiritual authority for people all over the world. In this specific section, you will read a particular passage of Scripture in preparation for the group meeting. Our conversation will focus on what we can learn from the passage and how it applies to our lives. So before we dive in, let's get acquainted with this ancient book.

The Bible contains a number of different books written by various authors. Turn to the Table of Contents for a list of all of them. Notice that there are two main divisions—the Old Testament and New Testament—and that the books often vary in length. For example, Psalms is the longest book of the Bible, while others like Obadiah are short and easily missed if you don't look carefully. The books themselves are divided into chapters and verses and often given abbreviations. For instance, Mt. 11:28 refers to the book of Matthew, chapter eleven, verse twenty-eight. A few short books do not have chapters and are only listed by their verses (Jude 15 refers to the book of Jude, verse fifteen).

The books of the Bible received their names for different reasons. Themes or central events were common. For example, Exodus concerns the deliverance of the Hebrew people from Egypt, and Acts describes the actions of early followers of Jesus. Some books were simply named after the authors (Luke), while others after a main character (Ruth) or prophet (Isaiah). In addition, a good portion of the New Testament is comprised of letters. Most were written from a person to a church or group of churches, though some were written to a particular individual. The names of a few books are distinguishable only by a number 1 or 2, as in a sequence or series of books. For example, 1 Thessalonians and 2 Thessalonians refer to two different letters the apostle Paul wrote to the church at Thessalonica.

STARTING POINT | chapter 1

Finally, the Bible combines an interesting variety of genres and literary styles. There is historical narrative, prophecy, proverbial sayings, legal material, poetry, songs, genealogy lists, letters, and even apocalyptic text—a special type of Jewish literature. Included are accounts of war, songs of celebration, prophetic speeches, tales of betrayal, encouraging letters, funeral dirges, and stories of love. There's something for everyone in this unique book. But most importantly, the Bible is the grand story of God and the people he created. And that makes it **your story** too.

QUESTIONS FOR REFLECTION:

■ What is one of your favorite stories and why do you like it?

■ Find 1 Samuel 17 in your Bible and read the famous story of David and Goliath. What makes it such a powerful story?

Small overcoming big

TENSIONS IN THE STORY

Does God really exist?

In Starting Point, we'll be talking about things like who God is and how to discover his will for your life. But those concepts are based on the conclusion that there *is* a God. Perhaps it's presumptuous to move ahead without first challenging the notion of God's existence. After all, who hasn't had doubts? It's only normal to wonder every now and then if we're all alone on this planet—whether there really is more to this life than this life.

The first thing to acknowledge in this discussion is that there's no way to *prove* or *disprove* God's existence. All anyone can do is present evidence. In reality, there's also no way to prove, beyond a shadow of a doubt, that the planet Jupiter exists, or that the Civil War actually happened, or that dinosaurs once roamed the earth. Granted, there's some very compelling evidence for all of those theses. But that's all it is—evidence. One of the limitations of human existence is that our perceptions of reality are confined to the five senses, the nature of logic, and the interpretation of the human mind. "Proof" is nothing more than evidence that results in a firm belief on the part of those who observe it.

That being the case, all we can do is examine the evidence for God's existence and draw our own conclusions. And as evidence goes, the claims that support God's existence are convincing. Philosophers propose that if everything in our world has a cause, then there must be an uncaused cause agent—God—who got the ball rolling. Scientists and physicists point to the order and design in the universe as evidence of an intelligent designer. Even ethicists assert that

STARTING POINT | chapter 1

our moral values must be based on something, or more accurately, on someone who sets an unchanging standard for right and wrong. In fact, the apostle Paul suggested that these moral bearings are written on our hearts by God himself (Romans 2:14-15).

Human nature itself also presents a long line of evidence for the existence of God. For starters, the concept of a deity seems to be woven into the human spirit. Virtually every culture throughout history has landed on that concept, along with the theory of an existence after this life. In addition, creation itself not only suggests that it was indeed created by someone, but it implies something about the abilities of whomever did it.

The most important evidence for God's existence can be found in the personal experiences of those who ponder the question. Life has a way of introducing various circumstances and obstacles that cause people to look outside themselves. And for those who are convinced of God's existence, they point to the evidence of his presence with them during those times as the most persuasive data. As David famously wrote: "Even though I walk through the darkest valley, I will fear no evil, for you are with me" (Psalm 23:4).

All of this may be why the Bible doesn't argue for God's existence, but just assumes it: "In the beginning God created the heavens and the earth" (Genesis 1:1). But regardless of your verdict at this point in your life, you are encouraged to continue seeking as we explore the grand story of our lives.

QUESTIONS FOR REFLECTION:

- What circumstances have caused you to believe or to doubt God's existence?

- How would you describe God's existence or presence in your life right now?

Doubt:
① When my dad went blind
② " my 1st husband cheated on me
③ When I couldn't conceive

Believe – ① Giving birth at 45
② Majestic oceans, sky, mountains

15

CONTINUING THE STORY

HERE ARE SOME ADDITIONAL PASSAGES IN THE BIBLE IF YOU WANT TO GO DEEPER:

Joshua 1:1-9 :: God promises his presence to Joshua as he embarks on a new journey.

Job 38:1-41 :: God chastises Job for doubting his existence.

Psalm 139:1-18 :: Our lives are in God's hands from the beginning.

Ephesians 1:15-23 :: Paul offers a prayer for those who are seeking God.

HERE ARE SOME OTHER SUGGESTIONS FOR FURTHER EXPLORATION:

 5 MIN. LISTEN to *Something's Missing* by John Mayer. "Something's missing and I don't know how to fix it."

 1 HR. SURF http://www.storycorps.net and listen to a few stories of everyday people. You might even want to record your own.

 1 HR. VISIT http://www.renderedartists.com to view a collection of artwork based on God's story.

2 HR. WATCH *The Truman Show* by Paramount Pictures, a captivating portrayal in which the protagonist plays the title character in the story of his own life.

 10 HR. READ *The Case for a Creator* by Lee Strobel, a compelling investigation of evidence for God's existence.

Go to http://www.startingpoint.com for additional resources.

STORYLINE OF CHAPTER ONE

- Each of our stories is part of a bigger story—God's story.

- As a group, we will explore the Bible together looking for guidance so you may find your place in the story.

For the Next Group Meeting:

- Read and complete the questions for Chapter Two and listen to the Chapter Two audio message.

- At the next group meeting, we will examine Scripture, the primary means by which God reveals himself and his story to us. Each time you meet with your group, you will reveal more of your story with the others. If given a specific opportunity to tell your story, how would you do it? Is it your style to keep it simple and recount a few milestones from your life? Or are you the creative type—possibly acting out a brief play about your life? Would you compile a soundtrack to describe your journey? Would you bring in pictures or other props for "show and tell"? Or would you share a funny or interesting story that captures the essence of who you are? During each meeting, we'll invite one or two people to share their life stories in their own creative ways. You'll need to be brief, but when the time comes, please be prepared to introduce yourself, highlight the pivotal events so far in your life, and share your spiritual journey using whichever method you choose.

GETTING THE *Script*

I believe the Bible is the best gift God has ever given to man.
~Abraham Lincoln

Truth only reveals itself when one gives up all preconceived ideas.
~Shoseki

Nobody ever outgrows Scripture; the Book widens and deepens with our years.
~ Charles Spurgeon

CHAPTER TWO

SCRIPTURE

Getting the Script

God reveals himself to us not in a metaphysical formulation
or a cosmic fireworks display but in the kind of stories that we use
to tell our children who they are and how to grow up as human beings.
~Eugene Peterson

Most people are bothered by
those passages of Scripture they do not understand,
but the passages that bother me are those I do understand.
~ Mark Twain

THE STORY UNFOLDS

The Story's Script

Our starting point begins with a question: If God wanted to reveal himself to humanity, how would he do it? How would he tell us his "story"? Perhaps he would paint a glorious picture in creation for all to observe. Or maybe he would put instincts in the human heart that point to his character. But perhaps more specifically, he might even provide a script that lays out the grand story of his reality and *our* purpose.

Whenever a subject like God or religion comes up, it's only a matter of time before the Bible is mentioned. It seems Christianity is permanently linked to the words recorded in this book. But why is that? For that matter, what is the Bible, exactly? And how did it come to be?

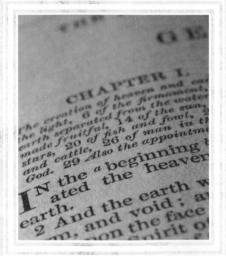

The Bible is the primary reference point for the beliefs of Christianity. As they live out their lives, people of faith look to Scripture for validation that their thoughts and actions are on the right track. That's a big assumption. And with so much riding on the contents of this ancient document, it's important to take a long, hard look at what this book is all about.

Technically, the Bible isn't one book. It's a library of books—sixty-six in all—compiled into one volume. Some of these books document historical events, while others are books of poetry, prophecy, or the laws of the people. Many are simply letters of instruction and encouragement addressed to various groups of people. And, of course, four of the books—Matthew, Mark, Luke, and John

THE BIBLE IS *the story of a loving God* WORKING TO DRAW PEOPLE TO HIMSELF.

collectively called "the Gospels"—provide detailed accounts of the life of Jesus. The first thirty-nine books of the Bible are referred to as the Old Testament—the part of the story from creation to the time before Christ. The remaining twenty-seven books make up what is called the New Testament, covering from the birth of Christ to the end of the story.

More than forty different writers penned the contents of the Bible over a period of more than a thousand years. Most never knew each other. And yet, when put together, these works form a consistent theme of a loving God working in the background to draw people to himself. Scripture is full of stories of human failure, violence, and rebellion. But God's faithfulness, patience, and forgiveness are always present behind the scenes. Is it possible, then, that God himself orchestrated the development and distribution of these writings so that we could find our places in his story?

QUESTIONS FOR REFLECTION:

■ What was your exposure to the Bible growing up?

Confirmation Study

■ How would you describe your current perspective on the Bible? What role, if any, does the Bible play in your everyday life?

Don't read often enough

None

THE STORY BEHIND THE STORY →■→

There are many ways to describe the Psalms, but first and foremost, they are prayers to God. They represent the honest longings of men and women who cried out to their heavenly Father. Fear, pain, confession, thanksgiving, and even celebration provoked these appeals. Sometimes they were sung with music when the Hebrew people gathered for worship. Other times they were simply prayed in the quietness of one's heart. But the Psalms were always significant, because they spoke not only of the human condition before God, but also of God's greatness in return.

Psalm 19 is a song of praise that celebrates the way God reveals himself to us. Initially, the writer praises God's revelation through the splendor of the heavens and the radiance of the sun. Nature communicates the story and the glory of God. But notice how the writer shifts gears. God not only reveals himself to us, but he reveals his purposes *for us*. And there is a place more perfect and radiant than creation to know God and his purposes: Scripture.

23

STARTING POINT | chapter 2

Read Psalm 19:1-11 in your Bible and respond to the following questions.

QUESTIONS FOR REFLECTION:

■ This Psalm moves from a description of creation to a discussion about Scripture. Why do you think the writer makes this comparison?

■ The Psalmist describes Scripture with words like *perfect*, *trustworthy*, and *right*. Does this seem overstated? Why or why not?

■ If you had the same convictions as the writer of this Psalm, what role would it play in your everyday life?

Why should I trust the Bible?

Some people are concerned that the Bible contains apparent contradictions and inconsistencies. After all, Scripture records historical events and sometimes the details don't jibe. Not to mention, it includes curious stories that seem to contradict the laws of science. In essence, people are asking, "Why should we trust the Bible?"

On one hand, the Bible possesses a significant amount of verifiable evidence to support its claims. Many parts of the Old Testament have been validated by archaeological discoveries such as the Dead Sea Scrolls. These well-preserved scrolls reveal the precision with which scribes copied and distributed Scripture. The accounts of the New Testament, including the life of Christ, are also extremely well-substantiated. That's because the existing manuscripts of the gospel accounts in today's museums date back further, are higher quality, and exist in much greater number than the earliest manuscripts of any other ancient document.

Nevertheless, some suggest that various passages of Scripture contradict one another. But scholars point out that a better grasp of the themes, language, culture, and original writings usually reveals that these so-called "contradictions" are only differences in emphasis. In fact, many point to the presence of apparent conflicts as evidence of authenticity because the variations are exactly what you would expect when two different people tell the same story.

25

STARTING POINT | chapter 2

Finally, some readers struggle with the scientific accuracy of Scripture.

Of course, biblical language was not meant to be scientifically precise. For example, ancient writers spoke of the sun rising and setting, just as we do today; but technically speaking, the earth rotates to reveal or hide the sun. On a similar note, some find it difficult to accept miracles. But if God created the universe and its laws, he certainly has the right to bend those laws from time to time. The question is whether we believe he can.

In light of the substantial evidence and these explanations, the Bible is trustworthy regarding the historical events it describes. The gospel writer Luke even defends his work by saying, "Since I myself have carefully investigated everything from the beginning, I too decided to write an orderly account... so that you may know the certainty of the things you have been taught" (Luke 1:3-4).

On the other hand, Scripture is so much more than a history book. It is a story. An unfolding story of creation, brokenness, promise, law, rebellion, grace, Spirit, and eternity. When we reduce the Bible to evidence and proofs, as important as those are, we miss the point. Ultimately, we have faith in the story because it draws us in, speaks to our lives, and nourishes our souls. One writer declares that Scripture "is a lamp to my feet and a light for my path" (Psalm 119:105). Yes, the story can be trusted, but the real issue is whether we can learn to trust its author.

QUESTIONS FOR REFLECTION:

■ Is it difficult to accept that the Bible is a historically reliable document? Why or why not?

No, but conflicting

■ Do you have trouble believing that the Bible is relevant to your life? Why or why not?

No, it is relevant

■ What would have to change for you to believe that the Bible is reliable and/or relevant?

Continuing the Story

Here are some additional passages in the Bible if you want to go deeper:

Nehemiah 8:1-18 :: A great celebration takes place when Israel rediscovers the Bible.

Isaiah 40:7-8 :: The prophet illustrates the endurance of God's Word.

2 Timothy 3:16-17 :: Paul writes about the origin of Scripture and its benefits.

Hebrews 4:12 :: The writer describes the power of God's Word.

Here are some other suggestions for further exploration:

 10 MIN. Surf http://www.startingpoint.com/bible for additional charts and explanation regarding the evidence for the Bible's reliability.

 2 HR. Listen to the entire sermon series *The Verdict* at http://www.startingpoint.com/audio

10 HR. Read *Is the Bible True: How Modern Debates and Discoveries Affirm the Essence of the Scriptures* by Jeffrey L. Sheler, a fair examination by a *U.S. News and World Report* journalist.

10 HR. Read *How to Read the Bible for All It's Worth* by Gordon D. Fee and Douglas Stuart; the title says it all.

Go to http://www.startingpoint.com for additional resources.

STORYLINE OF CHAPTER TWO

- The primary way God reveals himself to us today is through Scripture.

- The Bible is both historically reliable and relevant to our lives.

For the Next Group Meeting:

- Read and complete the questions for Chapter Three and listen to the Chapter Three audio message.

- At the next group meeting, we will discuss the beginning of the story: creation. As you prepare, think about one of the most beautiful places you have ever seen. Perhaps it was on a vacation or something you saw in a film. If you can, bring in a picture and be ready to explain to the group why it's beautiful to you.

The Story Begins

I love to think of nature as an unlimited broadcasting station, through which God speaks to us every hour, if we will only tune in.
~GEORGE WASHINGTON CARVER

God writes the gospel not in the Bible alone, but on trees and flowers and clouds and stars.
~MARTIN LUTHER

In wilderness I sense the miracle of life, and behind it our scientific accomplishments fade to trivia.
~CHARLES A. LINDBERGH

CHAPTER THREE

CREATION

The Story Begins

The sun, with all those planets revolving around it and dependent on it, can still ripen a bunch of grapes as if it had nothing else in the universe to do.
~GALILEO GALILEI

Look deep into nature, and then you will understand everything better.
~ALBERT EINSTEIN

Any patch of sunlight in a wood will show you something about the sun which you could never get from reading books on astronomy.
~C.S. LEWIS

THE STORY UNFOLDS ▪

The Big Idea

Sooner or later, we all hit the "big wall." It's the point in life when we realize that there has to be something bigger to life than living and dying. There has to be a big idea… a higher purpose. For some, it's a mid-life crisis, or the birth of their first child. For others it's a haunting question that follows them throughout their lives. But for all of us, it's an issue we must confront. What's it all for? Why am I here? What's the big idea?

Interestingly, everything about the world points us toward this question. We are surrounded by examples of bigness that leave us no choice but to feel small in contrast. Consider the night sky with its endless kaleidoscope of stars and planetary bodies drifting in clusters far beyond what our minds can imagine. Or our own ecosystem, which will sustain life for many thousands of years beyond what any of us will live. Or our bodies, which play host to thousands of microscopic miracles every time we take a breath or open our eyes or touch the hand of someone we love.

Our instincts and the *natural world around us* suggest that there is a master creator... *a big God.*

Deep inside, our instincts tell us that there's something bigger going on in the universe. We're not simply random bunches of molecules that assemble for seventy years and then die, eventually forgotten. Even the natural world around us suggests that there is a master Creator… a big God. And within his big purpose for his **creation**, we experience our greatest sense of purpose when we find our places in the story… his big story.

QUESTIONS FOR REFLECTION:

- When have you sensed that there is something bigger than you? Give examples.

- If God created everything, do you think he could be interested in the details of your daily life? Why or why not?

THE STORY BEHIND THE STORY →■→

Scripture begins with the story of creation. Naturally, this ancient Hebrew narrative raises more questions than answers. One is especially prone to wonder how the story of creation fits with recent scientific theories, an issue we will explore shortly. But don't miss the setting in which this account emerged. Other creation stories existed in the cultures of the ancient Near East. In them, many different gods ruled over chaos, and when they battled one another, skies and oceans and creatures were generated. Humans were an afterthought. Bored and hungry, the gods created people to fetch their food. Chaos, violence, and insignificance were the images of creation among many ancient peoples.

Genesis stands in stark contrast. The story begins with one God who creates humans to bear his glorious image. As you read the familiar account, don't overlook the rich imagery and poetic rhythm. Dwell on the magnitude of God's handiwork in each phase. Enjoy this picture of the world as it was meant to be.

CREATION   brokenness   promise

Read Genesis 1:1 through 2:3 in your Bible and respond to the following questions.

QUESTIONS FOR REFLECTION:

■ Do you find it hard to accept the story of creation? Why or why not?

■ What does this account reveal about God?

■ How does the creation of humankind differ from the rest of the account?

Is the creation account literal?

In writing, there are many different genres. Poetry is different from history, just as an editorial is different from prophecy. Interestingly, the Bible contains all of the above. So when it comes to a miraculous event such as creation, how should we interpret it? Did the author intend it as a literal account? Or was it just a metaphorical representation of the event? After all, we weren't there.

As you might imagine, many views have been presented over the years. Some scholars note that the creation story is more concerned with the "who" and "why" than the "what" and "how." Following this line of thought, they suggest that the account is a poetic summary of an elaborate series of scientific developments. Literalists, on the other hand, would disagree. They argue that events took place exactly as the text describes. In between, there are those who point out that God could use evolution as his method of creation. And finally, secular evolutionists leave God out of the picture altogether.

There are two challenges to this whole discussion. First, the human mind wasn't made to fathom an event of such magnitude. So for starters, we're playing out of our league (Romans 11:33-36). Second, there's just not enough scientific evidence to bring everyone's convictions into alignment. Until we come across additional information, the various sides will continue to argue their cases.

37

chapter 3

STARTING POINT

At any rate, certain facts are unmistakable in Genesis. Humans are the pinnacle of God's handiwork, created to reflect his image. What's more, creation didn't happen by itself. Many prominent scientists have eventually come around to this conclusion. So while we may not know precisely *how* our world came into being, Genesis tells us *who* brought it about (Genesis 1:1). And the marvels of our solar system point to a creative mind bigger than any human intelligence. The focus of our faith is the *Maker* of all **creation**, not the *method* of creation.

QUESTIONS FOR REFLECTION:

■ Of the different views on the creation of the world, which makes the most sense to you?

■ How important is it to you to know how human beings came into existence?

■ What has reading and discussing this creation account meant to you?

Joel Olstein
Proverbs 3:5-6 ; we can
not understand everything
the Lord does

CONTINUING THE STORY

HERE ARE SOME ADDITIONAL PASSAGES IN THE BIBLE IF YOU WANT TO GO DEEPER:

Psalm 33:6-9 :: This passage reminds us of God's great power.

Isaiah 40:1-31 :: Comfort is found in knowing that God is completely sovereign over the world.

Acts 17:22-28 :: In Athens, Paul makes a moving speech about God.

Romans 1:20 :: Paul states that we can all see something about God in creation.

HERE ARE SOME OTHER SUGGESTIONS FOR FURTHER EXPLORATION:

 5 MIN. SURF **http://www.startingpoint.com/powersof10**, an amazing depiction of creation.

 5 MIN. GOOGLE™ *Creation of Adam* by Michelangelo Buonarroti, an emotional portrayal of humanity's first moments.

 20 MIN. SURF **www.fullyrendered.com**, a collection of artwork inspired by the story of God.

1 HR. WATCH *Contact* by Warner Home Video. A scientist searches for meaning amongst the deep recesses of the universe.

 10 HRS. WATCH *Planet Earth* by the Discovery Channel®, a groundbreaking series about the wonders of the natural world.

Go to http://www.startingpoint.com for additional resources.

STORYLINE OF CHAPTER THREE

- The story begins with a glorious Creator and his beautiful **creation**.

- Human beings were created to reflect God's image and to be in a relationship with him.

For the Next Group Meeting:

- Read and complete the questions for Chapter Four and listen to the Chapter Four audio message.

- At the next group meeting, we will discuss what went wrong in the world, and unfortunately, what continues to go wrong. This week, as you scan the newspaper, read magazines, or surf the Internet, pay attention to all the terrible headlines. Choose one article that underlines the tragedies that exist in our world. Bring it to the next group meeting.

STARTING POINT | chapter 3

The
HUMAN tragedy

Our life is **full of brokenness**—
broken relationships, broken promises, broken expectations.
~Henri Nouwen

You have come into a hard world.
I know of only one easy place in it, and that is the grave.
~Henry Ward Beecher

Things aren't as bad as they seem. They're worse.
~Bill Press

CHAPTER FOUR

BROKENNESS

The Human Tragedy

If something can go wrong, it will.
~Murphy's Law

It is easier to denature plutonium
than to denature the evil spirit of man.
~Albert Einstein

THE STORY UNFOLDS

What's wrong with this picture?

Let's go ahead and admit it: the world is a messed up place. Brokenness abounds. Now, this doesn't mean we don't intend to have a positive attitude about it. There's a bright side to everything… things could be worse… we should be thankful for what we have… and all that. But just for the record, let's be honest about the general state of affairs on our planet. First of all, we have crime, pollution, erosion, and taxes—all of which seem to be on the increase. Then there's unemployment, disease, war, homelessness, and famine. Even the earth itself gets in on the mayhem, producing earthquakes, tsunamis, volcanoes, and hurricanes on a regular basis. Each of these disasters forms a stage on which a myriad of stories of human tragedy is played out. No words can capture the degree of human suffering that goes on each day in our world.

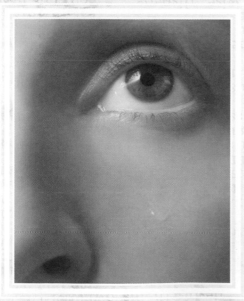

Innately, each of us recognizes that thing are not as they should be. When a child dies, we don't need someone to explain that it's abnormal. When someone cuts you off in traffic, instinctively you know that an offense has been committed against you. It seems we were born with a natural recognition of good and bad right and wrong. And as we look around us, things are definitely not right.

EACH OF US RECOGNIZES THAT THINGS *are not* AS THEY SHOULD BE.

So if a perfect God created an ideal world, then why's it such a messed up place? In the last chapter, we explored our universal desire for something more in life than what this world offers. And with all that's wrong in the world, is it any wonder we're left wanting more? This can't be it! Surely a supreme God wouldn't author a story so flawed… so anti-climactic… so broken?

It would be easy to sit around and complain, to cast blame on anyone and everyone for all the problems of this dysfunctional world. But if we're really honest with ourselves, don't we have to consider whether we're part of the problem? Each time we lose our temper, indulge our desire for control, or simply ignore someone else's cry for help, we contribute to the crisis. Somehow it's in our nature to be selfish—a nature we choose with every decision, and yet one we cannot seem to change. This is a sad story, indeed.

QUESTIONS FOR REFLECTION:

- What have you seen or read in the news lately that reminds you that the world is broken?

- What have you seen in your own life that suggests things are not as they should be?

Life in the garden was good for Adam and Eve. The environment was beautiful, animals were playful, and food was abundant. Of course, Adam and Eve also had one another, perfect companions. God had blessed them beyond all measure.

In light of this extraordinary provision, God asked a few things of the couple. First, they should "be fruitful." No complaints there. Second, they should rule over the earth. Not as dictators, but as good stewards who oversee and care for God's creation. Third, they could eat from any tree except one, the tree of the knowledge of good and evil. Partaking of it would bring a horrible consequence—death. And with no reason to doubt God, why would Adam and Eve want something that would harm them?

This is where the story takes a terrible turn. The following passage describes the fall of humanity into sin, which forever connects us to our first parents—both in their disastrous choice and the ensuing **brokenness**.

47

creation   BROKENNESS   promise   law

STARTING POINT | chapter 4

Read Genesis 3:1-24 in your Bible and respond to the following questions.

QUESTIONS FOR REFLECTION:

■ How would you describe the sin that Adam and Eve committed?

human Temptation
Greed
Curiosity

■ How did Adam and Eve's choice change the nature of their relationship with God?

Brought about guilt n shame
Separated
Guilt n shame

■ Why do you think God gave Adam and Eve the choice to disobey him in the first place?

TENSIONS IN THE STORY →■

Is sin really that big of a deal?

Sin is one of those universal concepts recognized in various cultures around the globe. Virtually everyone knows what it feels like to tell a lie, enjoy another's misfortune, or let anger run its course. In fact, sin is such an everyday occurrence, it's hard to imagine what the world would look like without it. We've learned to live with it. We've come to expect it. Some would even argue that the occasional sin is necessary to function in society. Sin has blended in. Which makes us wonder: Why is sin such a big deal in the Bible?

Since that day in the garden, sin has played a crucial role in our stories.

Sin is the great obstacle over which humans cannot seem to prevail. Sin uncovers the basic nature of humanity—that, in the end, we want things done our way—and reveals the epic challenge in our story. Sin is the boundary that tests our motives and exposes our frailties. No one is immune from the problem of sin. As one biblical author writes: "If we claim to be without sin, we deceive ourselves" (1 John 1:8).

God takes sin very seriously because of the statement it makes about our understanding of him. He is supreme. We are not. God is the ultimate authority. And we choose either submission to him or rebellion against him. One small sin may not seem like a big deal. But the nature of sin begs the question of whether we acknowledge God or not. And that's a big deal.

Declaring one tree in the garden "off limits" may seem arbitrary. Yet, Adam and Eve wanted to be like God rather than simply trust him. Ignoring the consequences of their decision, they defied God's authority. And when we sin today, we echo their choice by staging a one-person mutiny against the God of the universe. In a small way, our sin says, "I'll be my own god right now." By choosing sin, we demote God and put something or someone else in his place. And the brokenness that ensues reverberates throughout our lives and the lives of those around us.

Ultimately, the Bible says that sin results in death. The apostle Paul writes that "sin entered the world through one man, and death through sin, and in this way death came to all people because all sinned" (Romans 5:12). Sin causes death in our physical bodies and death in our relationship with God. Sin is a big deal. The important thing is not so much that we should succeed in avoiding it but that we acknowledge God as the one worthy of setting boundaries for us. The issue of sin, from a practical perspective, is the proving ground on which our loyalties are declared.

QUESTIONS FOR REFLECTION:

- In your own words, how would you define sin?

- How should we measure the seriousness of our sin?

- How do you respond to the statement that, like Adam ~~and~~ Eve, our sin has broken our relationship with God?

Handwritten notes:

Reacting vs Responding

Emotional "Rational"

Separation from God

Sin is disobedience against God

1-800- PRAY NOW

Wer	322-9099
Gon	749-9449
Dona	551-2306
Maxine	652-8190
Jeavette	439-8957
Cili	418-4137
Nancy	673-8180

Continuing the Story

Here are some additional passages in the Bible if you want to go deeper:

Genesis 4:1-12 :: This is the story of Cain and Abel; it's all downhill after the garden episode.

2 Samuel 11:1-27 :: Even the best (King David) can do the worst (deception, adultery, and murder).

Psalm 51:1-7 :: David confesses the depth of his sin and his need for restoration.

Romans 7:18-24 :: Paul verbalizes a struggle we've all experienced.

Here are some other suggestions for further exploration:

 5 MIN. GOOGLE™ *The Scream* by Edvard Munch, a haunting painting by the Norwegian artist

 5 MIN. LISTEN to *Grey Street* by Dave Matthews Band. "There's an emptiness inside her and she'd do anything to fill it in."

 2 HR. WATCH either *Schindler's List* by Universal Studios or *Hotel Rwanda* by MGM, disturbing depictions of human depravity.

 5 HR. READ *Lord of the Flies* by William Golding, an allegorical novel suggesting what happens when humanity is left to its own devices.

Go to http://www.startingpoint.com for additional resources.

■ The world is broken because humanity chose to defy God by satisfying our selfish desires.

■ The result of our sinful nature is death—both physical death and death in our relationship with God.

For the Next Group Meeting:

■ Read and complete the questions for Chapter Five and listen to the Chapter Five audio message.

■ At the next group meeting, we will discuss how God responds to a broken relationship with humanity. All of us, from time to time, experience alienation from people who have been important to us. What would it take to reestablish one of these relationships? Do you have someone from whom you've disconnected? **Would you consider taking the first step to initiate reconciliation?** This week, be bold and make the first move to pursue reconciliation. Be prepared to share with your group the outcome, as well as your emotions during the process.

STARTING POINT | chapter 4

The First *Move*

God loves each of us as if there were only one of us.

~St. Augustine

For however devoted you are to (God), you may be sure
that he is immeasurably more devoted to you.

~Meister Eckhart

God's promises are like the stars;
the darker the night the brighter they shine.

~David Nicholas

CHAPTER FIVE

PROMISE

The First Move

[God] is not proud...He will have us
even though we have shown that we prefer everything else to Him.

~C.S. Lewis

It is much more possible for the sun to give out darkness than for
God to do or be, or give out anything but blessing and goodness.

~William Law

The First Move

So the world's a messed up place. And as we saw in the last chapter, there's something missing inside us because of it. We're not only disconnected from each other, we're disconnected from our Creator. And as long as we remain in that state, it's impossible for us to experience the fullness of life. Thank goodness our story doesn't end there. Our Creator knows we need to reconnect. So despite our relentless disinterest in him, God made the first move to reestablish his connection with humankind. And that part of the story really begins to unfold with a man named Abraham.

Abraham lived in the Middle East in about 2000 BC. He was an old man with no children, and, therefore, no hope of a family legacy. In those times, a man without a legacy was viewed as having lived a meaningless life. As if to exploit irony, God chose this unlikely man to become the ultimate patriarch... the surrogate father of God's own plan for reconciliation. To Abraham, God would not only grant a son, but through him, God would begin a long lineage of descendants that would eventually affect all humankind.

Interestingly, God announced this plan to Abraham in the form of an emphatic promise. It wasn't a "Hey, wouldn't it be nice if someday..." kind of comment. It was a bold declaration. And in light of their prospects for children, it sounded so preposterous to Abraham's wife that she laughed out loud. Nevertheless, God was making a promise, and the promise

GOD MADE THE FIRST MOVE TO REESTABLISH
his connection with humankind.

was to make a point. *In the midst of a chaotic and uncertain world, there is such a thing as certainty.* And God was introducing himself as the source of that certainty.

Even today, it seems there are no guarantees in the world. We aren't guaranteed a job, or a family, or our health. And the whole point of Abraham's story is that God's promises are the one place where we can find absolute certainty in the world. History shows that God fulfills his promises and when you think about it, they are the only fixed reference points we have. If you base your life on a career or a relationship or a standard of living it's just a matter of time before uncertainty creeps in. Even the future of our planet seems questionable at times. But time after time, the promises of God have proven to be reliable.

And when it comes to reconnecting with our Creator, God's promises emerge as our one true source of certainty. God has responded to the problem of sin with a **promise** for all humanity. We can connect with him. He made the first move.

QUESTIONS FOR REFLECTION:

■ Describe the last time someone promised something to you and let you down.

■ Based on your perception of God, do you feel he can be trusted? Why or why not?

Life was different for Adam and Eve outside the garden. It didn't take long for sin to manifest itself in terrible ways. Cain savagely killed his brother; others followed his example by settling disputes with bloodshed. Selfishness ruled. And as the human population grew, so did sin and death. One ancient story says that God judged the rampant evil by causing a great flood and purging the world of wickedness. In his mercy, God spared one righteous man and his family, but even Noah's sinful nature got the best of him. It seemed that no descendant of Adam and Eve was immune from the infection of sin.

Indeed, neither time nor correction could reverse the curse. Humanity had rejected its Creator. The relationship between God and humans was utterly ruined. Just when it could get no worse and when it appeared that his only solution was to abandon creation altogether, God did something amazing. Making a promise to one man, God whispered the story of humanity's redemption.

59

creation

brokenness

PROMISE

law

rebellion

Read Genesis 12:1-3 and 15:1-6 in your Bible and respond to the following questions.

QUESTIONS FOR REFLECTION:

■ If you were God and humankind had rejected you, how would you have responded?

■ What was God promising to Abraham? Why would God make such a sweeping promise to one person?

■ Why do you think Abraham trusted God?

Tensions in the Story

How much faith do I have to have?

So, there's something compelling about the idea of connecting with God and living in a relationship with him. Maybe you're thinking it holds some merit for your life too. But then you read an amazing story about the faith of a person like Abraham and you think, "I could never do that." Or you look at some of the Christians around you and conclude, "I'm just not like them. I mean, I might believe this stuff. But frankly, some of it sounds kind of bizarre… even unrealistic." At the root of these thoughts is an important question: How much faith do I have to have?

Do you have to be like Abraham in order to seek a relationship with God? Do you have to surrender *everything* before you can gain *anything*? Our culture emphasizes things like speed, progress, and comparison. So it's only natural to wonder how we measure up compared to other people. But God's love isn't so generic. When he pursues a relationship with you, it's not a formula derived from a lofty moral standard. He wants you. And that includes all your apprehensions and hesitations. Like the man who said to Jesus, "I do believe; help me overcome my unbelief!" (Mark 9:24), you don't need any more faith than what you have.

We tend to think of faith as an uncomfortable, blind leap. But in reality, faith means choosing what is real, although unseen, over what is seen. And when you experience it, faith actually shows up in the form of new desires in our hearts, not the fearful prospect of facing something we dread.

You'll know it's true faith when your desire to follow the will of God begins to reshape your old desires. Faith is simply choosing the new desire over the old—God's way over the old way.

Hebrews 12:2 refers to Christ as "the pioneer and perfecter of faith." That means God not only made the first move, but he also knows how to move it along. We just need to stay interested in exercising whatever faith we possess in the moment. Has he given you a measure of faith already? What would it look like for you to move forward in that faith… to take a step of faith? Remember you don't have to understand *everything* to believe in *something*. You may not understand how a computer works, but that doesn't mean you can't check your email. And just because you've never rebuilt an engine, it doesn't mean you can't drive to work. Faith is never a factor of quantity. It's simply a matter of applying what we do understand and trusting God to keep his promise…to take us the next step when the time comes.

QUESTIONS FOR REFLECTION:

■ What does the word "faith" mean to you?

■ Do you ever feel that all your doubts must be erased before you can trust God?

■ In what areas of your life do you find it most difficult to trust God?

CONTINUING THE STORY

HERE ARE SOME ADDITIONAL PASSAGES IN THE BIBLE IF YOU WANT TO GO DEEPER:

Genesis 15:7-21 :: God makes a covenant with Abraham, pledging to fulfill his promise.

Proverbs 3:5-6 :: Solomon offers wise advice about the nature of faith in God.

Luke 15:1-32 :: Jesus tells three parables to illustrate the amazing love of God the Father.

Hebrews 11:1-40 :: Read about heroes of faith from the Old Testament.

HERE ARE SOME OTHER SUGGESTIONS FOR FURTHER EXPLORATION:

 5 MIN. LISTEN to *All Because of You* by U2. "You heard me in my tune, when I just heard confusion."

 10 MIN. GOOGLE™ *The Starry Night* by Vincent van Gogh. "Look up at the heavens and count the stars, Abraham..."

2 HR. WATCH *Finding Nemo* by Walt Disney, an animated underwater adventure depicting a father's relentless search for his son.

 10 HR. READ *Abraham: A Journey to the Heart of Three Faiths* by Bruce Feiler. A Jewish journalist investigates what people of three major religions believe about this mysterious man of the Bible.

Go to http://www.startingpoint.com for additional resources.

■ God responded to the problem of sin with a promise that demonstrated his desire to restore his relationship with humanity.

■ Like Abraham, we can trust God's promises.

For the Next Group Meeting:

■ Read and complete the questions for Chapter Six and listen to the Chapter Six audio message.

■ Next week, we will examine the emergence of Israel as a nation and the rules that God gave them. Keeping rules is no easy task. The desire to do things our own way is both strong and persistent. Between now and the next group meeting, your assignment is to *obey all traffic laws to the exact letter of the law*. Pay attention to any attempts to justify deviating. Is there a benefit to following the rules? Is it possible to do everything right?

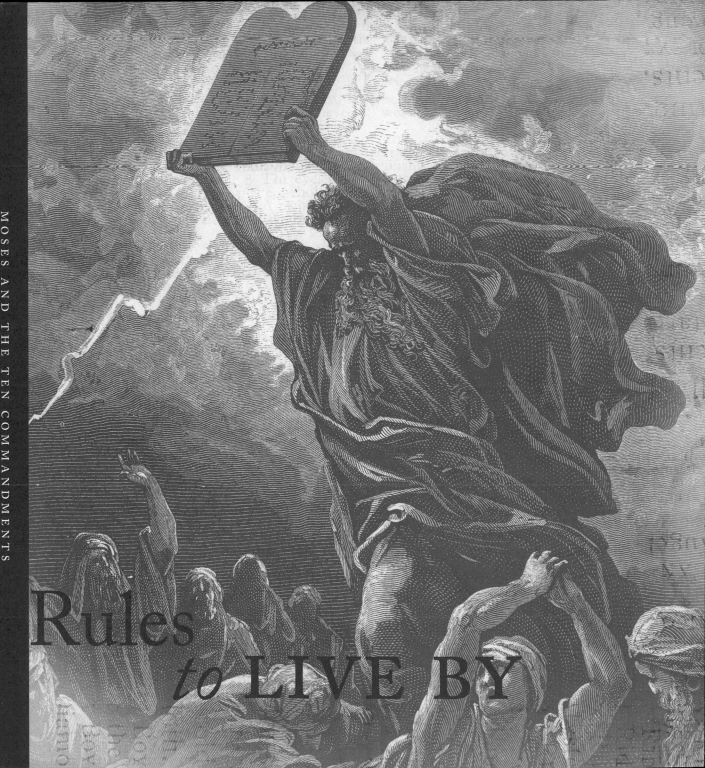

MOSES AND THE TEN COMMANDMENTS

Rules *to* LIVE BY

Where there is no law, but every man does what is right in his own eyes,
there is the least of real liberty.

~HENRY M. ROBERT

Law means good order.

~ARISTOTLE

It may be true that the law cannot make a man love me,
but it can keep him from lynching me, and I think that's pretty important.

~MARTIN LUTHER KING, JR.

CHAPTER SIX

LAW

Rules to Live By

The purpose of the law is to prevent injustice from reigning.
~FREDERIC BASTIAT

We may not all break the Ten Commandments, but we are certainly all capable of it.
Within us lurks the breaker of all laws, ready to spring out at the first real opportunity.

~ ISADORA DUNCAN

The Purpose of Rules

There's an unspoken belief that shows up in many world religions. It is the belief that acceptance by God is dependent on keeping a set of rules. Whatever the faith, there seems to be a universal understanding that God is good, people are bad, and in order to approach God, therefore, we must first live up to his standards. We must find a way to be good. But while that may be the stated belief of some religious people, it has never been the case with the God of the Bible. In fact, the opposite is true. Our ability to obey a set of rules has no impact on our ability to approach God. In a painful irony, it's likely that throughout history this one distortion has done more to alienate people from God than any other factor.

By nature, rules can never be the foundation of a mutual relationship. Rules may be the foundation of imprisonment or slavery. But if a relationship is to be based on free choice, rules can never be more than an addition to it—not the basis for it.

In the last chapter, we saw that God made the first move to reestablish a connection with humankind through a promise given to Abraham. The fulfillment of God's promise began when he delivered Israel from slavery and gave the new nation a legal code. At the centerpiece of this law was the Ten Commandments. Ever since, it seems the human race has wrestled with its sense of worthiness before God.

GOD NEVER INTENDED FOR *rules to be a measure* OF OUR ACCEPTABILITY.

But God never intended for those rules to be a measure of our acceptability. They were an expression of his character. And there's a big difference. After all God had done to establish his people, there was no question that they were acceptable to him. And as their God, it was only natural that they reflect his values in their society. With the law as the foundation for their government, Israel could be God's light to all the other nations. God's rules were not a condition for a relationship, they were the confirmation of one.

QUESTIONS FOR REFLECTION:

■ What were the rules like in your home as a child or teenager?

■ When do you keep rules and when do you tend to break them?

THE STORY BEHIND THE STORY →■⟶

Just when creation appeared doomed to failure, God initiated an epic plan. Through Abraham, God would produce a great nation and ultimately bring his gracious favor to all peoples of the earth. Most of Genesis follows the story of Abraham's family. Abraham had Isaac, Isaac had Jacob, and Jacob had twelve sons. Eventually, the entire family moved to Egypt where Abraham's descendants grew into a multitude. Threatened by their numbers, Pharaoh enslaved the Hebrew people. And so became the plight of Israel, a nation in slavery and bondage for hundreds of years.

As the people cried out to God, he heard their pleas and delivered them. In the familiar story, Moses confronted Pharaoh and God demonstrated his power over Egypt through ten terrible plagues. Leading them out of Egypt and protecting them along the way, God brought Israel to Mt. Sinai where he gave them the law. The following narrative records the heart of God's instruction to his people.

creation   brokenness   promise   LAW   rebellion   grace

Read Exodus 20:1-21 in your Bible and respond to the following questions.

QUESTIONS FOR REFLECTION:

■ What would the world look like if everyone obeyed the Ten Commandments? If everyone *disobeyed* the Ten Commandments?

■ What makes a rule good or bad?

■ What happens when people get too focused on keeping laws and miss the purpose of laws?

Why is God so concerned with rules?

Mention God and what's the first image that comes to mind? For many people, God is floating around his holy throne room monitoring video screens like the night watchman for morality. Whenever he spots a violation, he dispatches his special agents—the God squad—to send a corresponding measure of destruction and mayhem into the perpetrator's life. His job is to punish failure. And when he's not enjoying a little retribution, he passes the time making up more rules to catch us falling short.

It's easy to see how God's reputation gets linked to rules. Many of the major headlines from the Bible involve stories of forbidden fruit, tablets of stone, and ceremonial laws that rival the choreography of a Broadway show. So at first glance, it's no wonder God gets labeled as the supreme legislator.

But when you look beyond the façade, there's more to God than just a cosmic stop sign. Yes, God is concerned with rules. But not for the reasons we might think. Rules serve some very practical purposes in the universe and for each person in it. And as the chief caretaker, God knows their value all too well. For starters, rules reveal what's important and what's not. They point us away from danger and show us the route to safety. And while nobody enjoys conforming to restraints, that doesn't mean it's not a good idea. A seat belt may wrinkle your dress, but consider the alternative.

Second, rules tell us a lot about the Rule Maker. If you want to know what's valuable to God, just examine the rules he established and what they're designed to protect. For instance, God communicated to Israel that he values honesty (Deuteronomy 25:13-16), healthy relationships (Leviticus 18:1-24), and concern for the poor and marginalized (Exodus 22:21-25).

And finally, rules help us see what we're made of: they test our character. For a good look in the mirror, notice what rules you tend to break and which ones are easy to keep. Ultimately, rules help settle once and for all the question of whether or not we're good, and they point the way to our need for grace and forgiveness.

Rules give us navigational cues for understanding God and advancing through life. And when you consider that God never introduced his law apart from the context of an intimate relationship, it's clear that God is more concerned with protecting us than limiting us. More importantly, rules not only reflect God's character—they reveal ours.

QUESTIONS FOR REFLECTION:

- Is it fair for God to give us rules? Why or why not?

- Which rules do you associate with God that are hard for you to keep?

CONTINUING THE STORY

HERE ARE SOME ADDITIONAL PASSAGES IN THE BIBLE IF YOU WANT TO GO DEEPER:

Exodus 11:1 – 12:13 :: The Passover is a defining event for Israel.

Leviticus 16:1-34 :: The law included provisions for lawbreakers.

Psalm 105:1-45 :: God initially fulfills his promise to Abraham through Israel.

Matthew 22:34-40 :: Jesus summarizes the heart of the Old Testament law.

HERE ARE SOME OTHER SUGGESTIONS FOR FURTHER EXPLORATION:

 5 MIN.   GOOGLE™ a picture of *Jebel Musa,* the probable location of Mt. Sinai, where Moses received the Ten Commandments.

 2 HR.   WATCH *The Prince of Egypt* by Dreamworks. This animated film captures the heart of the biblical story.

 3 HR.   LISTEN to the entire sermon series *The Sinai Code* at http://www.startingpoint.com/audio.

 10 HR.   WATCH Krzysztof Kieslowski's *The Decalogue* by Image Entertainment, a series of ten short films examining the complexity of human sin against the backdrop of the Ten Commandments.

Go to http://www.startingpoint.com for additional resources.

Storyline of Chapter Six

- God gave the law to the Israelites so that they could reflect his character and recognize their shortcomings.

- Keeping God's law is not a condition of a relationship with him, but a confirmation of one.

For the Next Group Meeting:

- Read and complete the questions for Chapter Seven and listen to the Chapter Seven audio message.

- At the next group meeting, we will discuss Israel's defiance of the Ten Commandments and the law. As we examine their rebellion, consider how you too have rebelled against God. This week's exercise will be challenging. Spend some time alone thinking about the way sin manifests itself through your thoughts and actions. **Using pen and paper, write down your most selfish ways, habits, and behaviors.** It can be in the form of a confessional prayer to God or a simple list. Fold it up and put it in a sealed envelope. Be honest, because no one else will see or read what you write. Bring your list and envelope to the next group meeting.

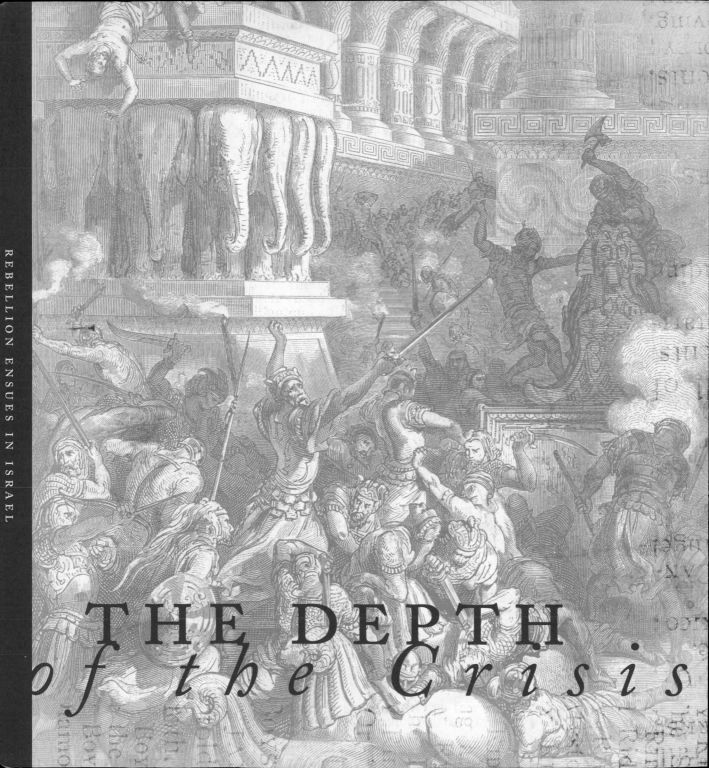

THE DEPTH
of the Crisis

Mankind have **banned the Divinity** from their presence; they have **relegated him to a sanctuary;** the walls of the temple restrict his view; **he does not exist** outside of it.

~Diderot

The more **laws and order** are made prominent, the more thieves and robbers there will be.

~Lao Tzu

Let's just say I was **testing the bounds** of society. I was just curious.

~Jim Morrison

CHAPTER SEVEN
REBELLION

The Depth of the Crisis

The central idea of the great part of the Old Testament may be called the idea of the **loneliness of God.**

~G. K. Chesterton

Israel is the **bearer of the solution** to the world's ills; but Israel has itself become **part of the problem.**

~N.T. Wright

The Problem With Rules

We admitted that the world is not the way it is supposed to be. Now it's time to admit our roles in the misfortune. You see, it's impossible to take an honest look at God's universe without also being honest when we look in the mirror. We're not just innocent bystanders. We're part of the human race notorious for messing the place up. And while you might not be the one who ate that first apple in the garden, we all have our passion fruit. And when the situation is ripe, we'll indulge ourselves at the expense of what is good and right.

Now don't take this the wrong way. This is not a rebuke of your character and a call to better morality. We simply want to see things for what they are. Everybody's a rebel. Perhaps not compared to the people around you. But when held up to the light of God's standards, we're all guilty of various forms of rebellion. We've all sinned. Some have said the devil made them do it. But more likely, there's something about rules that makes us do it. Draw a line and the temptation is to cross it. There's a dark corner inside every human heart that would rather know what it's like to break the rules than to live safely within them.

Granted, when an inventor breaks the rules, it's a good thing. But violating God's laws always leads to pain and

Our *rebellious nature* CAUSES SEPARATION FROM GOD.

destruction. Relationships are damaged. Fortunes are ruined. Lives are destroyed. But even worse, our rebellious nature causes separation from God.

The consequences of our rebellion are all around us. And they go far beyond mere crime and social dilemmas. According to the Bible, sin introduced the world to concepts like death, suffering, and the savage side of nature. But all of these are just symptoms of the real problem. We are cut off from God. The rebellion that led to Adam and Eve's eviction from the garden exists inside each of us. And unless something is done about it, we are heading deeper and deeper into crisis.

QUESTIONS FOR REFLECTION:

- Why is it easier to identify sin in other people than it is to recognize it in ourselves?

- Do you think of yourself as having a rebellious nature? Why or why not?

THE STORY BEHIND THE STORY

After God gave Israel the law, they settled in Canaan, where tribal infighting and chaos was the norm. Local judges ruled until about 1000 BC, when Israel crowned Saul as their first king. David and his son Solomon followed, establishing Israel as a great and mighty kingdom in the ancient Near East. After Solomon's death, civil war ensued and the nation split into the southern kingdom of Judah and the northern kingdom of Israel.

During this divided era, many kings ascended to the thrones of Judah and Israel. Most were selfish and power-hungry. They fought against one another, negotiated foreign alliances with corrupt nations, and abandoned their worship of God. Following their leaders, the Hebrew people turned to pagan idols and defied God's law. Enter the prophet Jeremiah to call God's people to account for their **rebellion**. Instead of modeling God's character, Israel had become a nation of rebels. The bearers of God's solution were part of the problem.

83

REBELLION

law

grace

spirit

promise

Read Jeremiah 2:1-13 in your Bible and respond to the following questions.

QUESTIONS FOR REFLECTION:

■ What do you think Jeremiah meant with the imagery of "broken cisterns"?

■ In what ways could God have responded to Israel's rebellion? To yours?

■ Have you ever had someone speak into your life when it was off track? What was your response?

Tensions in the Story

Why does God seem so different from the Old Testament to the New Testament?

It is widely accepted that the God of the Old Testament threw tantrums and hurled brimstone whenever his people failed to measure up. Meanwhile, the God of the New Testament is portrayed more like a loving, merciful grandfather who spoils his grandchildren at Christmas. So what could have triggered such a major transformation? Did God get counseling in anger management? Or is he just so old that he can no longer remember what made him upset in the first place? There must be an explanation.

As with any assumption, it's a good idea to challenge its premise before we embrace it. If you think about it, many of our mental images are based upon random, innocuous sources that were never intended to tell the whole story. That's how urban myths get started. So when it comes to our mental images of God, it's worth a closer look at where we get our information and how we process it.

There have been thousands of commentaries on God's nature through the years. Artists have depicted him in museums using oil and canvas. And loiterers have described him on street corners using the gift of gab. There's such a diversity of information about God, it's hard to know what to believe. Fortunately, we have an authorized biography, including details about his interaction with the very first people and predictions of how he'll deal with the last. So there's little need to speculate. And while there are stories that show God's wrath in the Old Testament, there are similar stories throughout the New Testament (Acts 5:1-11 and 9:1-4). Likewise, God's gentler side isn't confined to the New Testament. He is equally characterized using words like *grace* and *compassion* in the Old Testament (Exodus 34:6-7 and Jonah 4:2).

In fact, the closer you examine the evidence, the more it suggests that God's nature has remained consistent throughout time. He has always had the potential to face evil with wrath. And he's always had the propensity to show mercy toward those who ask for it. Throughout the Bible, he is depicted as showing amazing patience in the face of cruel rejection. There's no doubting his love for us. One New Testament writer calls him our "Father of the heavenly lights, who does not change like shifting shadows" (James 1:17). God's character hasn't changed. Our depiction of him has.

QUESTIONS FOR REFLECTION:

- Where does your mental picture of God come from?

- How accurately do you think your image of God reflects what you are learning about him in the Bible?

- How do you think God will respond if you admit your rebellious ways to him?

Continuing the Story

Here are some additional passages in the Bible if you want to go deeper:

Nehemiah 9:1-37 :: During one of Israel's revivals, they come clean about their rebellion.

Isaiah 1:1-20 :: The prophet highlights Israel's rebellious ways and issues an ultimatum.

Matthew 23:1-39 :: Jesus gives his harshest remarks to the religious leaders of Israel.

Mark 1:1-8 :: The last great prophet prepares Israel for a final solution to their rebellion.

Here are some other suggestions for further exploration:

 5 MIN. GOOGLE™ *Christina's World* by Andrew Wyeth; a young woman experiences alienation from that which she loves.

 5 MIN. LISTEN to *Born to Be Wild* by Steppenwolf or *My Life* by Billy Joel, anthems of rebels

10 MIN. WATCH *NOOMA Sunday* by Rob Bell, a video about what God wants from us; purchase at http://www.startingpoint.com/sunday.

2 HR. WATCH *Thirteen* by 20th Century Fox, a story about a teenager's rebellion and devastating consequences that follow.

Go to http://www.startingpoint.com for additional resources.

■ Israel's **rebellion** exposed the depth of the sin problem.

■ When we rebel, we isolate ourselves from a relationship with God.

For the Next Group Meeting:

■ Read and complete the questions for Chapter Eight and listen to the Chapter Eight audio message.

■ Bring your "Rebellion" list and envelope from the last chapter to your next group meeting.

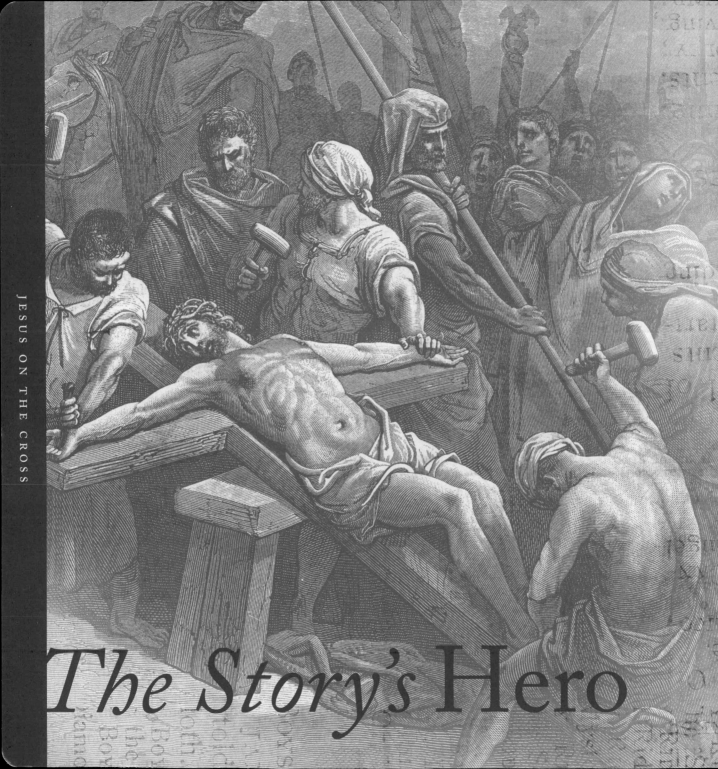

The Story's Hero

If our greatest need had been information, God would have sent an educator.

If our greatest need had been technology, God would have sent us a scientist.

If our greatest need had been money, God would have sent us an economist.

But since our greatest need was forgiveness, God sent us a Savior.

~Roy Lessin

The dying Jesus is the evidence of God's anger toward sin;
but the living Jesus is the proof of God's love and forgiveness.

~Lorenz Eifert

CHAPTER EIGHT

GRACE

The Story's Hero

I do not at all understand the mystery of grace - only that it meets us where
we are but does not leave us where it found us.

~Anne Lamott

Grace is not a license to sin, but to walk in humility in the sight of God.

Grace frees us to be active in the works of God.

We are not tied up with how much we have done, or not done,
but we learn by the grace of God to rest in His love.

~Curt McComis

There Must Be Some Mistake

"What goes around comes around." "You'll get yours someday." "It all evens out in the end." You've probably heard those sayings all your life. And to a large extent, they represent a basic belief shared by most people. There's an instinctive voice of reason inside each of us that describes a cause-and-effect relationship between how we behave and how we will fare. We may cheat the system temporarily. But intuitively, we all tend to anticipate a final hearing in which justice will eventually be served.

So it's no wonder we're taken aback when the opposite occurs. Once in a while it happens. A shopper breaks an expensive collectible, but the store owner tells her not to worry about it. Someone openly jilts a co-worker, only to have the same person recommend him for a promotion. A motorist rear-ends another driver, but the victim dismisses the damage as only a scratch—not worth bothering about.

In spite of our relief in a situation like that, there's something completely unnatural about accepting those terms. Our internal scoreboards blow a circuit. Deep inside, we resist it. "It can't be right," we think. "There must be some mistake."

OUR MANY OFFENSES *warrant full condemnation for our sins*, BUT GOD OFFERS TO PAY THE PENALTY HIMSELF.

God's **grace** *strikes us the same way.* While our many offenses warrant full condemnation for our sins, God offers to pay the penalty himself. In Jesus, God became flesh, lived a sinless life, and offered himself as a sacrifice on a cruel Roman cross; the Creator of the universe, dying for the sins of humanity, then conquering death on behalf of all who identify with him. Through the person of Christ, God has posted full bond on our behalf. We're set free to live the life for which we were created.

QUESTIONS FOR REFLECTION:

- Describe the most extreme act of forgiveness you've ever witnessed or experienced.

- Do you feel that you deserve God's love and forgiveness?

Despite the impassioned pleas of the prophets, Israel's rebellion continued. In time, the Assyrians and Babylonians carried off the Hebrew people into exile. A remnant of Jews returned, but Israel had seemingly failed to portray God's favor to the world. As centuries passed, some Jews hoped for a Messiah who would make all things right, but many were dismayed by God's apparent silence. The outlook for humankind was bleak.

Then one day, a new Rabbi appeared, teaching with powerful authority. He spent time with the poor and downcast, even prostitutes and nobodies. Stories of miraculous healings circulated, and people—even women and non-Jews—began to seek him. Some called Jesus the long-awaited Messiah.

95

rebellion   GRACE   spirit   eternity

Religious leaders worried. Jesus announced the arrival of a new era of liberation, forgiveness, and God's kingdom—declarations only God could make. Their authority and traditions challenged, these powerful leaders resolved to silence Jesus. While he was in Jerusalem for the Passover Feast, they put him on trial for blasphemy. What took place next defines not only Jesus' life, but the story of God's grace and humanity's redemption.

Read Matthew 27:1 through 28:20 in your Bible and respond to the following questions.

QUESTIONS FOR REFLECTION:

- In this narrative, what was unique about what Jesus said or did? What he did not say or do?

- What does Christ's death mean to you personally?

- Do you think Christ's resurrection is important to the story? Why or why not?

TENSIONS IN THE STORY

Don't all religions lead to God?

The similarities between various world religions are striking. First of all, there's the basic concept of a supreme god. Even when multiple deities are worshiped, religions often acknowledge one particular god as preeminent. Second, they agree that this divine being can be either loving or wrathful, depending on the circumstances. And finally, the notion that this god requires something from humankind is represented in virtually every case. In some comparisons, the similarities between belief systems are downright uncanny.

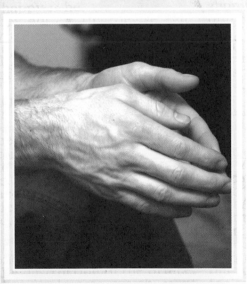

All this begs the question: is it possible we're all describing different paths to the same god? After all, we may sound a little different, but we all have voices. We may be colored a little different, but we all have skin. So if we have slightly different ways of approaching our particular god, is that so wrong?

In reality, the differences between Christianity and other religions far outnumber the similarities. Judaism bears the closest resemblance, right down to the promise of a Messiah who would restore people to God and reverse the curse of brokenness in our world. But when Jesus came as the Messiah, he was rejected by the leaders of that religion.

What Jesus did and taught also separates Christianity from all other religions. He asserted: "I am the way and the truth and the life. No one comes to the Father except through me" (John 14:6). Thus, God's plan for humanity, which began with a promise to Abraham, reached its climax in the death and resurrection of Christ. Jesus was not only the Messiah of Israel, but the Son of God and Savior of the world. This is why his early followers asserted: "Salvation is found in no one else, for there is no other name given under heaven by which we must be saved" (Acts 4:12). While many other religions contain positive teachings and enlightening insights, only Jesus offers forgiveness of sin and reconciliation with God. Therefore, dismissing him is to decline the very grace God has extended.

Ironically, many still attempt to earn God's favor through the same efforts at performance that resulted in our failure with God to begin with. Thus, other religions have been defined as humanity's effort to get right with God. Whereas Christianity has been described as humanity's reliance on God's effort—namely, the work of Christ. There is a famous passage that describes the nature of God's grace:

"For God so loved the world that he gave his one and only Son, that whoever believes in him shall not perish but have eternal life. For God did not send his Son into the world to condemn the world, but to save the world through him" (JOHN 3:16-17).

These verses give a detailed explanation of the purpose behind Christ's life, death, and resurrection.
The motive was that God loved the world. The highlight is that God gave his Son. The response is that we believe in him. And the result is that we receive eternal life.

In summary: God loved. God gave. We believe. We receive.

QUESTIONS FOR REFLECTION:

- Why does it matter which religion a person chooses?

- If all religions lead to God, why do you think God would have sent Jesus to die such a horrific death on our behalf?

- What is your response to this summary?

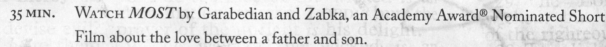

HERE ARE SOME ADDITIONAL PASSAGES IN THE BIBLE IF YOU WANT TO GO DEEPER:

Isaiah 53:2-12 :: The prophet foretells Jesus' amazing sacrifice.

Matthew 5:1-7:29 :: Jesus delivers his famous Sermon on the Mount.

Romans 5:6-8 :: At the perfect time, Christ died for us.

Philippians 2:5-11 :: Paul summarizes the person and work of Jesus.

HERE ARE SOME OTHER SUGGESTIONS FOR FURTHER EXPLORATION:

 5 MIN. GOOGLE™ *The Return of the Prodigal Son* by Rembrandt, a beautiful interpretation of the famous parable.

 35 MIN. WATCH *MOST* by Garabedian and Zabka, an Academy Award® Nominated Short Film about the love between a father and son.

 2 HR. WATCH *The Passion of the Christ* by Fox Home Entertainment, a graphic interpretation of the final hours in the life of Jesus, scripted almost directly from the Gospels.

2 HR. WATCH *Les Miserables* by Victor Hugo, a story of revenge and redemption toward a reformed prisoner.

 10 HR. READ *The Jesus I Never Knew* by Philip Yancey; discover a Jesus different than the one history and religion have distorted.

Go to http://www.startingpoint.com for additional resources.

STORYLINE OF CHAPTER EIGHT

- Our rebellion warrants full condemnation, but in his grace, God offers to pay the penalty for us.

- When we express faith in Jesus' death and resurrection, our relationship with God is restored.

For the Next Group Meeting:

- Read and complete the questions for Chapter Nine and listen to the Chapter Nine audio message.

- Next week, we will continue exploring what it means to have a relationship with God. Specifically, we will discuss God's presence in our lives through the Holy Spirit. Before the next group meeting, set aside 15-30 minutes one day to simply listen for God's "voice." Go somewhere different from your normal routine. Take a walk. Or maybe just sit in that room of the house you never use. Leave everything else behind for a few minutes and give your attention to God. Offer your worries up to him. Ask his Spirit to guide your thoughts. And plan to share your experience with your group.

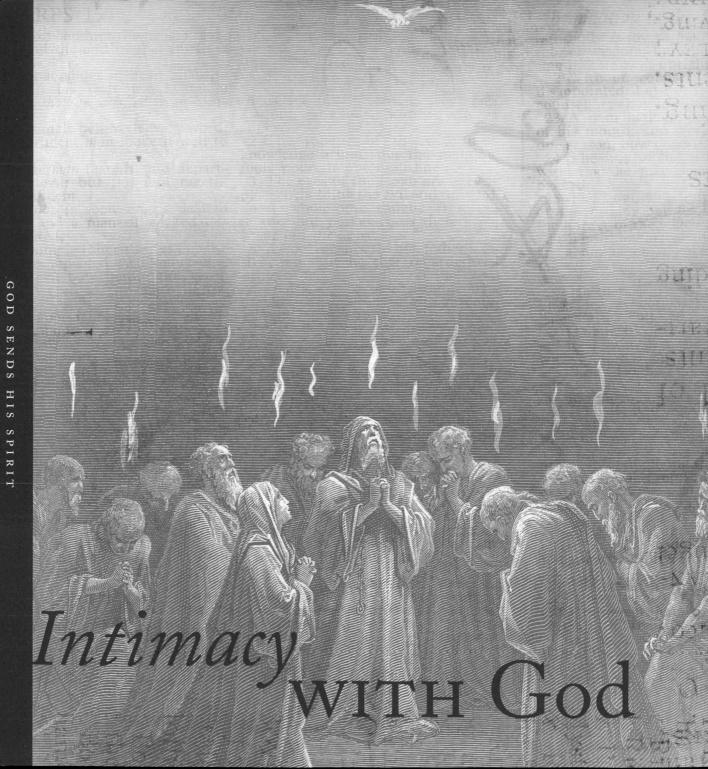

Intimacy WITH God

You stir man to take pleasure in praising you,
because you have made us for yourself, and our heart is restless until it rests in you.
~St. Augustine

I just go where the life is, you know? Where I feel the Holy Spirit.
~Bono

We are not human beings on a spiritual journey.
We are spiritual beings on a human journey.
~Stephen Covey

CHAPTER NINE
SPIRIT
Intimacy With God

The knowledge of God is very far from the love of Him.
~Blaise Pascal

Those who believe they believe in God but without passion in the heart,
without anguish of mind, without uncertainty, without doubt, and even at times
without despair, believe only in the idea of God, and not in God himself.
~Madeleine L'Engle

A Still, Small Voice

In addition to physical needs like food and water, humans must also have certain relationship needs met in order to thrive. These needs underscore the importance of intimacy in our lives. We all need to be known authentically and accepted for who we are. People are spiritual beings. And the quality of our interaction with others directly impacts our quality of life. Wealth, good looks, talent… no matter how abundant our other assets, nothing makes up for a deficit of intimacy. Needless to say, one of our deepest longings is to establish intimacy with the God who created us and loves us.

There's just one problem. How can we have meaningful interaction with a God we can neither see nor touch? The disciples must have wondered the same thing when Jesus left. The time they spent with their leader made them feel closer to God than ever before. Then one day, he was gone. Once the experience of meeting together was over, they must have wondered if they'd ever feel that close to God again. Only afterward did they learn that God's plan was actually to send the Holy Spirit to guide, correct, comfort, and encourage them. Jesus had referred to him as the "Counselor" who would live inside them. And despite the fact that Jesus was gone, the disciples managed to experience intimacy with God when they listened and followed the promptings of that still, small voice in their hearts.

GOD HAS GIVEN US THE *Holy Spirit*
TO WALK THROUGH LIFE *with us.*

That's the plan for God's intimacy with you too. And ironically, it's probably not to different from the subtle promptings that led you to seek him out through this small group. Just as God' Spirit was able to lead you then, he will continue to guide you wherever you go. One day, Christ himse will come back in person. Until that time, God has given us the Holy Spirit to walk through life wit us. So our intimacy with God is not based on keeping a list of rules. As a member of God's family, yo have God with you… in you… as a still, small voice and a powerful force. Thus living your life with Go is simply a matter of following him whenever prompted. And while it's not the same as interacting wit a visible person, we can learn to listen for God's Spirit speaking into our lives.

QUESTIONS FOR REFLECTION:

■ When have you sensed a "still, small voice" guiding your life? Describe.

■ How can you know if it's really God's voice you're hearing? Share your suggestions.

THE STORY BEHIND THE STORY ■→

Following his resurrection, Jesus ascended into heaven. Soon after, God's Spirit empowered the small band of believers, and thousands of Jews placed their faith in Jesus. Others came to understand that in Christ, God was offering reconciliation to all people. This good news spread like wildfire. New converts were baptized and gathered into local communities of faith. They read Scripture, prayed, and shared meals together. Believers also met to worship God and remember Christ's death through communion. It wasn't long before the movement reached every corner of the Roman Empire.

Before his death, Jesus prepared his followers for what was about to take place. He reminded them that the focus of their faith was a relationship with God. And spreading God's love to others would only be a result of experiencing it first themselves. Knowing that he would be leaving, Jesus promised to send someone else. Intimacy with God would be found by walking in step with the Holy Spirit.

107

eternity

SPIRIT

grace

rebellion

STARTING POINT | chapter 9

Read John 14:1–27 in your Bible and respond to the following questions.

QUESTIONS FOR REFLECTION:

■ What do you find most intriguing about the Holy Spirit?

■ Is the title "Counselor" a helpful description for the Holy Spirit? What are some other ways you would describe him?

■ What causes you to doubt the Holy Spirit's presence in your life?

How can I know God's will for my life?

Not long after you start your journey toward God, a common question arises: What's next? As you begin to trust God and his plan for your life, it's only natural to wonder what to do next. You've seen what it looks like to pursue your own will. But what exactly does it look like to follow God's will? Ephesians 2:10 says that "we are God's handiwork, created in Christ Jesus to do good works." How can you be sure you won't miss any of your assignments?

You can read the Bible and find out what to do about sin. You can listen to a sermon and get a general idea of how to treat people. But when it comes to making decisions about the direction of your life, what should you do?

109

Recognizing God's will may be easier than it seems. With the Holy Spirit as your internal guide, you can be certain that God will be working in all things together to bring about his plan for you—even if you fail along the way. Paul assures us that "he who began a good work in you will carry it on to completion" (Philippians 1:6). Since God made the first move toward us, he will be faithful to lead us in every part of his will for our lives. But what does that look like? And what can you do to be certain you hear him?

There are several methods God consistently uses to grow your faith and help you discern his will. Here are a few:

- ❖ Practical Teaching – reveals where we are and where we need to go.
- ❖ Providential Relationships – allow us to hear from God through others.
- ❖ Private Disciplines – tune our hearts to God's heart.
- ❖ Pivotal Circumstances – force us to look to God.
- ❖ Personal Ministry – enables us to experience God's power.

God's will rarely comes to us in the form of a detailed script. But as we learn to walk in step with the Holy Spirit, we find guidance for day-to-day living. These five catalysts play a significant role in finding God's will, growing in your faith, and developing intimacy with your Creator.

QUESTIONS FOR REFLECTION:

■ How could the Holy Spirit work through each of these five catalysts?

■ Which of these catalysts has God used recently to grow your faith or direct your path? Share an example.

■ Which catalyst has had the least impact on your spiritual journey?

Continuing the Story

Here are some additional passages in the Bible if you want to go deeper:

Psalm 139:7-12 :: There is nowhere we can go where God's Spirit is not present with us.

Romans 8:9-17 :: Paul deeply expounds the benefits of the Holy Spirit in our lives.

Galatians 5:16-26 :: Paul explains what life is like with and without the Holy Spirit.

Philippians 3:7-11 :: Everything else is rubbish compared to intimacy with Christ.

Here are some other suggestions for further exploration:

 5 MIN.   LISTEN to *Yahweh* by U2, a prayer to God for a transformed life.

 2 HR.   LISTEN to *Ignite*, a sermon series at http://www.startingpoint.com/audio.

10 HR.   READ *Sacred Pathways* by Gary Thomas; everyone has his or her own unique way of drawing near to God.

 10 HR.   READ *The Life You've Always Wanted* by John Ortberg, an introduction to practicing private disciplines.

Go to http://www.startingpoint.com for additional resources.

■ We can grow in intimacy with God by keeping in step with his Spirit.

■ God has given us the Holy Spirit to guide, correct, comfort, and encourage us.

For the Next Group Meeting:

■ Read and complete the questions for Chapter Ten and listen to the Chapter Ten audio message.

■ Reflect on your Starting Point group experience. You've explored your faith in light of God's story. You've also met some new people who may have challenged you in new ways. For the final group meeting, make a few notes in the space below about how you've grown spiritually and how others in the group have influenced your progress.

113

STARTING POINT | chapter 9

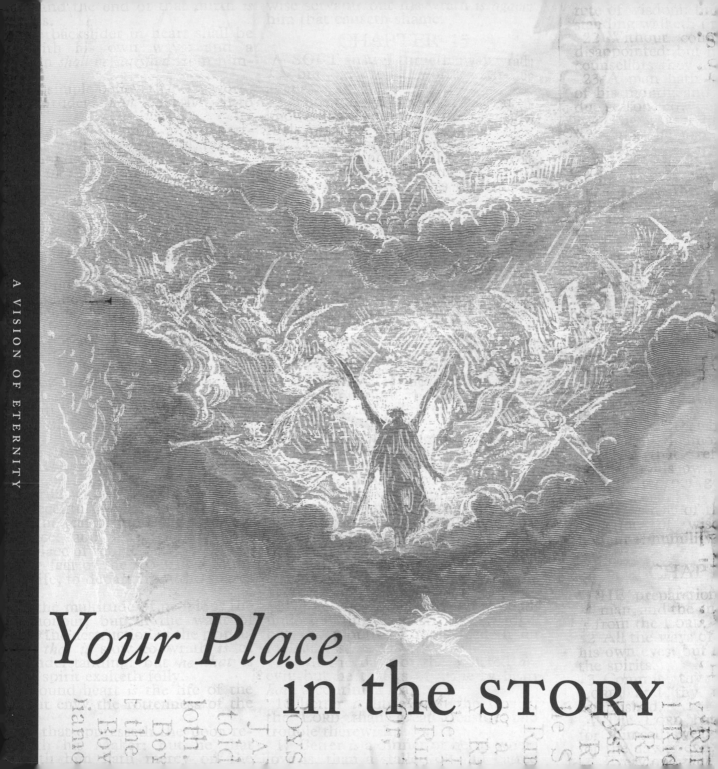

Your Place in the STORY

Story is the most adequate way we have of accounting for our lives, noticing the obscure details that turn out to be pivotal, appreciating the subtle accents of color and form and scent that give texture to our actions and feelings, giving coherence to our meetings and relationships in work and family, finding our precise place in the neighborhood and in history.
~Eugene Peterson

We shall not cease from exploration
And the end of all our exploring, Will be to arrive where we first started
And know the place for the first time.
~T.S. Eliot

CHAPTER TEN

ETERNITY

Your Place in the Story

The greatest thing is to be found at one's post as a child of God, living each day as though it were our last, but planning as though our world might last a hundred years.
~C. S. Lewis

The answer to the question "Who am I?" can only be given if we ask "What is my story?" and that can only be answered if there is an answer to the further question, "What is the whole story of which my story is a part?"
~Lesslie Newbigin

The Rest of the Story

You can tell a lot about people by how much they think abou retirement. Those who ponder it a lot are either old or diligent; and those who don't are either young or foolish… or both. As a general rule, people are not very good at planning for the long-term. If event are too far out in the future, they seem irrelevant. Why not just cross that bridge when you get to it?

Well, just when you've mustered up the courage to write down your goals, there's a new long-term pictur to start preparing for. Eternity. Ironically, most people believe in the concept of the afterlife. But fev know how to prepare for it. After all, preparing for the future requires that we have an accurate pictur of where we're headed.

Just as it's important to plan for retirement the evidence suggests that we should b planning beyond as well. Everybody lives forever And when you really examine the story of us, it's clear tha the storyline points to a place called eternity. The whole picture in God's story—and in yours—ends with a climacti reunion scene. At last, we will finally be united again… th way it should be.

In the meantime, we express our hope for that day when w pursue intimacy with God and community with others who are on the same journey. Together, all are united in the work

WHEN YOU REALLY EXAMINE *the story of us*, IT'S CLEAR THAT THE STORYLINE POINTS *to a place called eternity.*

of preparing for the final kingdom that is to come. It is that mission that unites your small group of fellow sojourners, your local community of faith, and the global church in the same pursuit.

All this leads to an important question: What is your place in the story?

It is to live in constant fellowship with God and to pursue his will for each moment; to attune yourself to the language of the Holy Spirit; to boast only in the cross of Christ; to integrate with other believers in the community of God—all so that you may participate in the story of the church making disciples of all nations... until the end of time.

QUESTIONS FOR REFLECTION:

- How has your understanding of the purpose of your life changed over the years?

- How should the concept of eternity shape your decisions in life?

The New Testament records the accounts of Jesus' life and the early church.
Chronologically, it concludes sometime in the late first century AD. Since then, history has borne witness to shining examples of Christian love, as well as tragic episodes of disgrace. Despite instructions for living found throughout Scripture, God's people have always struggled to find the balance between truth and grace, belief and action, and present and future.

The book of Revelation is different from most other books in the New Testament. First, it was a letter to persecuted churches and, therefore, should be read in light of their historical circumstances. Second, it contains prophecy, like many Old Testament books. And third, Revelation resembles other writings from the ancient Near East called apocalyptic literature. This means that it uses wonderful imagery and a cosmic narrative to portray God's ultimate consummation of history. For us—it is a vision of **119** eternity that provides hope for the future and purpose for the present.

ETERNITY

spirit

grace

Rebellion

STARTING POINT | chapter 10

Read Revelation 21:1 through 22:21 in your Bible and respond to the following questions.

QUESTIONS FOR REFLECTION:

■ Have you experienced anything in this life that resembles how this writer depicts heaven? Describe.

120

■ In this passage, what do you think it means for God to "wipe every tear from their eyes"?

■ Does this vision of eternity seem unrealistic to you? Why or why not?

TENSIONS IN THE STORY

What happens after death?

If there's one question common to all generations and all cultures, it is the question of the afterlife. In pyramids and on cave walls, humankind's fascination with our mortality has been well-recorded. We can't help wondering what happens when we die. And today's readers of the Bible are no exception. Sure, we have a general idea of what takes place. Heaven is supposed to be great. Hell is supposed to be bad. But most of us envision little more than winged versions of ourselves flying among the clouds and playing various instruments. So what should we expect?

One of Jesus' last conversations before death was with two dying men. These thieves were being crucified on either side of him. One of the men simply mocked Jesus. But the other believed Jesus was God's Son. He appealed to him, "Jesus, remember me when you come into your kingdom" (Luke 23:42). Like many of us, this man sensed he would continue on after death, and he wanted the mercy only Christ could give.

Jesus gave the penitent man clear reassurance: "Truly I tell you, today you will be with me in paradise" (Luke 23:43). The word "today" assured the thief of an immediate transfer from this life into heaven. No waiting around for the end of time. No holding pattern. His soul instantaneously present in God's company. The Greek term for paradise, *paradeisos*, is derived from a Persian word that describes an enclosed park, a shady grove, or a pleasure ground. The Bible doesn't tell us everything about heaven, but the point is pretty clear—it's sure to be a blissful place. So blissful that the apostle Paul says "we… prefer to be away from the body and at home with the Lord" (2 Corinthians 5:8).

The Bible also points to a later time when Jesus will return to earth and bring history to its consummation. Justice will finally be served and peace will prevail. Everyone will be evaluated for his or her faithfulness in working for God's kingdom. With resurrected bodies, a "new heaven and a new earth" will become our final destination (Revelation 21:1).

In the end, the million-dollar question won't be "What happens after you die?" but "What happened as you lived?" Eternity has begun. And those who find their places in God's story will spend it with him forever.

QUESTIONS FOR REFLECTION:

■ What is your mental image of life after death? What sources contributed to your picture?

■ How should our view of eternity influence how we live?

■ How do you intend to continue your pursuit of finding your place in the story?

CONTINUING THE STORY

HERE ARE SOME ADDITIONAL PASSAGES IN THE BIBLE IF YOU WANT TO GO DEEPER:

Isaiah 65:17-25 :: Long ago, God promised to make all things new one day.

Titus 2:11-14 :: In view of Christ's return, we become a people of mission.

2 Peter 3:10-15 :: Peter draws some clear conclusions about the meaning of life and faith.

Revelation 5:1-14 :: A vision of heaven includes people from all nations worshiping God.

HERE ARE SOME OTHER SUGGESTIONS FOR FURTHER EXPLORATION:

 5 MIN. GOOGLE™ *Peaceable Kingdom* by Edward Hicks, one artist's depiction of the world to come.

10 MIN. READ *Death, Be Not Proud*, a sonnet by John Donne about hope for a coming day when death itself shall be no more.

10 MIN. WATCH *NOOMA Trees* by Rob Bell, a video about God's story; purchase at http://www.startingpoint.com/trees.

2 HR. SURF http://www.thehopevideo.com, a depiction of God's redemptive story from beginning to end.

10 HR. WATCH *The Lord of the Rings* trilogy by New Line Home Entertainment, an epic story of the battle between good and evil.

Go to http://www.startingpoint.com for additional resources.

STORYLINE OF CHAPTER TEN

■ Each of our stories is a part of a bigger story—God's story.

■ In light of **eternity**, your task is to find your place in the story.

After Your Group Ends:

■ Read the Epilogue.

■ Celebrate both the journey on which you have been and the journey on which you are embarking.

■ Connect with a long-term small group where you can continue to explore faith and experience community.

Before the world began, God existed.

He created the universe to his liking… beautiful and full of life. As if to crown his handiwork, he breathed life into man and woman and put them in charge of the earth. They were born to enjoy God's presence. By their own nature, they received God's love… and loved him in return. *Creation*.

But soon, their freedom became their undoing. By choice, they deliberately defied God's wishes. No longer unified in spirit, the two existed separately—God in his holy place, and humanity in a world now spoiled. *Brokenness*.

Blind to the relationship that once was, later generations groped for a solution to the disarray they had inherited. When the time was right, God began to make himself known once again. First through a vow to one man: Abraham. *Promise*.

As the centuries unfurled, God's promises were faithfully realized. A nation rose up bearing the favor of the one, true God. His commandments were like guardians, protecting them from harm. *Law*.

Kings, priests, and prophets followed. And generation after generation tested the patience of their God. Despite his unceasing mercy and compassion, they repeated the defiance of the first man and woman. *Rebellion*.

Then, in a climactic gesture of restoration, God donned human flesh and walked the earth. He subjected himself to the depravity and ignorance of the people he loved… even to the point of death.

As a final demonstration of his authority, he rose from the dead, presenting himself as the means of redemption for anyone who would receive him. *Grace*.

Many followed him. By his presence, he empowers those who remain dedicated to the continuing work of reconciliation. They walk in step with the voice of God living inside them. *Spirit*.

One promise remains. That he will return one day, make all things new, and reunite once again with those who choose him. *Eternity*.

Epilogue

And so we come to the end of the beginning. Through Starting Point, you have begun a dynamic conversation that will likely last you a lifetime. It is an engagement that connects you with God and with others. Hebrews 10:25 encourages us to consider "not giving up meeting together…." You too must continue to seek out this vital experience in the future. You have learned a valuable process that gives you access to the ultimate meaning and purpose for your life. Personal fulfillment is realized when we pursue spiritual growth in a conversational environment where God's truths are esteemed.

Starting Point is designed to be a place where it's safe to ask any question about God and faith. And just because your group has completed this study, it doesn't mean you will no longer have questions. In fact, as you continue to investigate the story, you are likely to encounter more questions than you had before. Eventually, we hope that you will be comfortable not only searching for the answers yourself, but also helping others in their journeys. In the meantime, please don't hesitate to ask your Starting Point leader for guidance regarding any of your curiosities or concerns.

Your Starting Point experience has introduced you to the value of exploring faith in a community setting.

Hopefully, you have been able to share in meaningful conversations about the story of God and humanity. And by now, you should be more confident about continuing the mission of finding your place in the story.

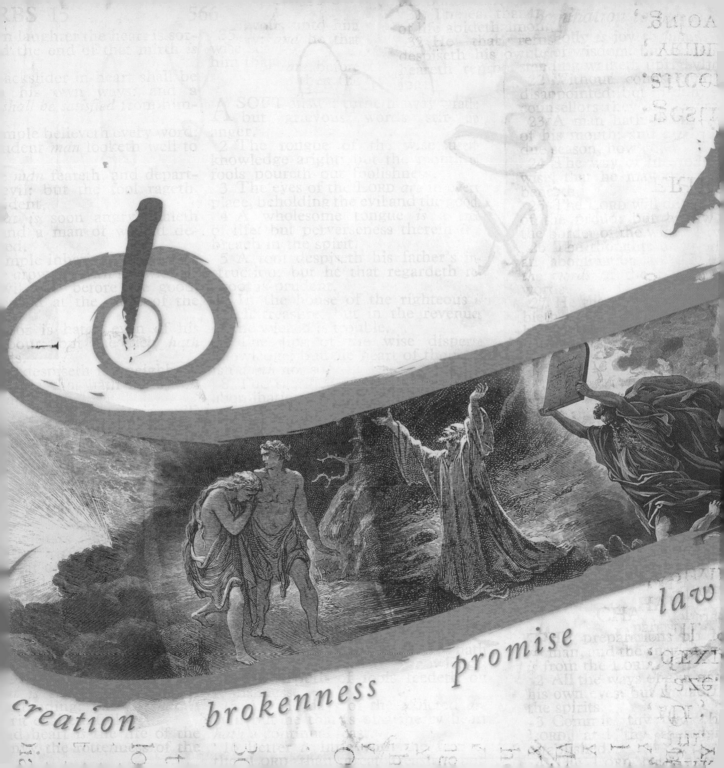

creation   brokenness   promise   law

rebellion grace spirit eternity

O<small>NCE</small> upon a time . . . .

A Note From Andy Stanley

When our friends at Zondervan agreed to partner with us to distribute our Starting Point materials to a broader audience, they asked if I would allow my name to be printed on the cover. From a publishing perspective, they were convinced this new product needed to be easily identifiable with North Point and that adding my name would be the easiest way to accomplish that. After some debate, I agreed. But to be honest, it still feels a bit uncomfortable. We've been creating Starting Point materials for eight years and never thought to put anyone's name on the cover. Starting Point is a collaborative effort that began in 1997. Dozens of men and women have participated in the creation and re-creation of this incredible tool. So it is only fitting that I give credit where credit is actually due.

Jason Malec, who serves as the director of Starting Point, drove the process in developing this current edition. His passion to engage starters, seekers, and returners in meaningful conversations around issues of faith drove him to take our existing Starting Point curriculum and create an experience that would take participants beyond a typical group study. Thank you, Jason.

Working closely with Jason was Norton Herbst, who did the lion's share of the writing and editing. Norton's unique insights and gifting are displayed throughout this work. Along with Jason and Norton, I want to thank others who participated on the Starting Point curriculum team: Erin Caprielian, Michael Colwell, Steve Giddens, Lisa Leeman, Tracey Scholen, Jeff Gribble, Ben Ortlip, Randy Walton, and Bill Willits.

A special thank-you to Lane Jones and Sean Seay for creating our first Starting Point curriculum, as well as launching our initial Starting Point groups over ten years ago. Without your vision and hard work, this current edition would not exist.

Finally, I am extremely grateful for all of our Starting Point leaders at North Point Community Church, Buckhead Church, and Browns Bridge Community Church. You have provided invaluable insight and input throughout the process. You are the heartbeat of Starting Point. Thanks to your tireless leadership and availability, countless seekers, starters, and returners continue to find their places in the story.

Disc 1

Disc 2

Disc 3